D1465979

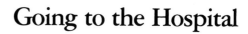

Going to the Hospital

Going to the Hospital

BY FRED ROGERS

photographs by Jim Judkis

The Putnam & Grosset Group

With special thanks to: Nan Earl Newell;
Margaret B. McFarland, Ph.D., Senior Consultant;
Michael B. Rothenberg, M.D., Mary Donnelly, M.S., and
Beverley H. Johnson, Consultants; Barry N. Head;
the Dubner family; Claire McLamore, Tom McLamore,
and Gail Thomas; Children's Hospital of Pittsburgh;
and the other parents and children who agreed
to help us with the book.

Text and photographs copyright © 1988 by Family Communications, Inc.
All rights reserved. This book, or parts thereof, may not be reproduced
in any form without permission in writing from the publisher.
A PaperStar Book, published in 1997 by The Putnam & Grosset Group,
345 Hudson Street, New York, NY 10014.
PaperStar Books is a registered trademark of The Putnam Berkley Group, Inc.
The PaperStar logo is a trademark of The Putnam Berkley Group, Inc.
Originally published in 1988 by G. P. Putnam's Sons.
Published simultaneously in Canada.
Manufactured in China
Library of Congress Cataloging-in-Publication Data
Rogers, Fred. Going to the hospital. (A Mister Rogers' First experience book)
SUMMARY: Describes what happens during a stay in the hospital,
including some of the common forms of medical treatment.
1. Children—Hospital care—Juvenile literature.
2. Children—Preparation for medical care—Juvenile literature.
[1. Hospitals. 2. Medical care.] I. Judkis, Jim, ill. II. Title. III. Series: Rogers, Fred.
Mister Rogers' First experience book. RJ242.R64 1988 362.1'1 87-19170
ISBN 978-0-698-11574-3

When children have to go to the hospital, it can be a hard time for them, as well as their parents and other people who take care of them. One reason we made this book was to show children what hospitals are like, and we hope the words and pictures will be helpful in that way.

Another reason for this book, though, was to give you and the children in your care a way to talk about going to the hospital and about some of the feelings adults and children both have when hospitalization occurs. Talking together is one of the best ways to make feelings manageable. As you trust one another with those feelings, you may find that talk turns into play. Play is something we always encourage because it is one of children's most important ways to get used to the idea of something new—especially when it's something new that could be scary.

People who love children hate to have them very sick or badly hurt, but there are things we adults can do when such times come. We can remind ourselves that those times are not our fault. We didn't make our child sick or hurt. And we can give our children the best care we know. Sometimes that means taking them to the hospital. Since we adults have feelings, too, we need to be gentle with ourselves as well as with our children as we all prepare for any first experience in our life. We can't possibly anticipate every aspect of hospitalization for our children, but showing them that it's all right to talk about the kinds of things that *might* happen is a healthy beginning.

However you choose to use this book, we hope it will help you and the children you care for all grow together through times that may be hard.

—Fred Rogers

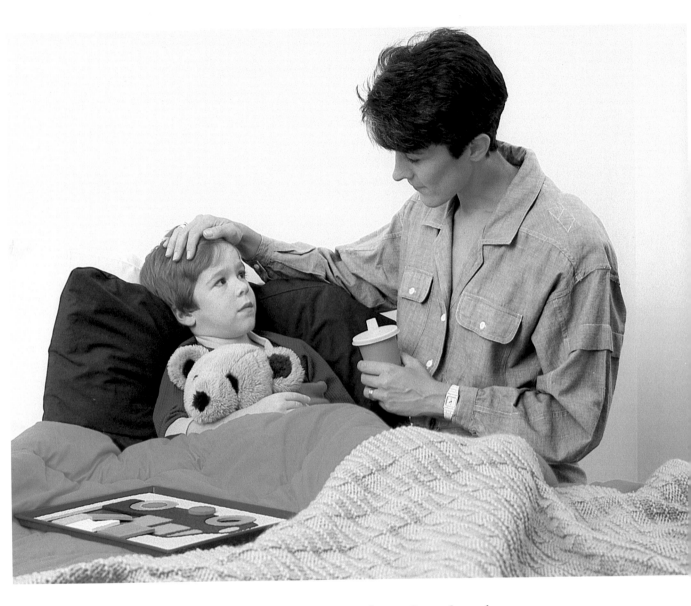

Have you ever had to stay in bed for a few days because you were sick or hurt? Many children have times like that—times when their moms and dads help them get well at home.

There are times, though, when children need care that their moms and dads can't give them at home. Those are times when parents may have to take their children to a hospital.

A hospital is a place where doctors and nurses
work together with others to take special care
of people who are sick or hurt.

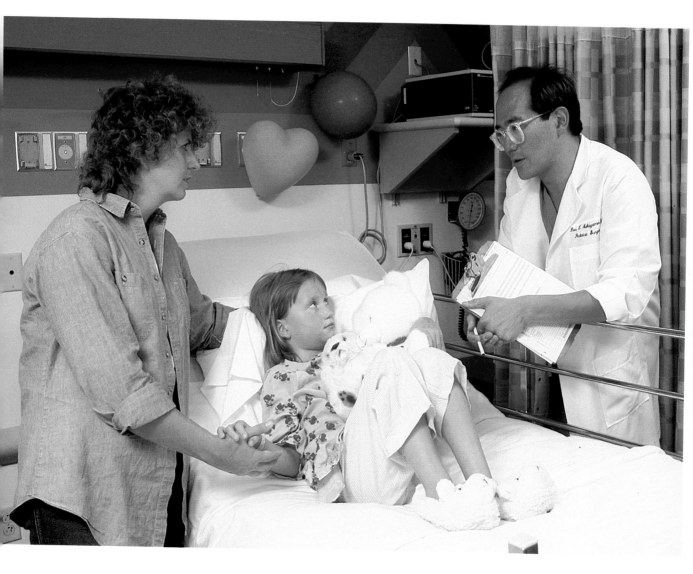

When people go to the hospital, they might stay for a day or they might stay for several days. No matter why you go to the hospital or how long you stay, you'll get to go home again just as soon as the doctor decides you're well enough to leave.

When you're getting ready to go to the hospital, there's lots to do and plenty to think about. You might want to ask questions about why you're going to the hospital, and what it will be like there. You might want to play about it, too.

If you're going to the hospital for only a day, you may want to bring along your favorite toy. But if you're going to stay for more than a day, you'll probably pack a bag with things you want to have with you . . . like pajamas, slippers, a toothbrush, a favorite book or toy, and clothes to wear when you come home. Some people like to take along a picture of their family, too.

People have lots of different feelings about going to
the hospital. Some even think that it's their own fault
that they're there. But it's *not* their fault. Going to
the hospital isn't a punishment—it's a way of getting
help. If you're feeling sad, or scared, or angry, it
can help to tell someone you trust how you're feeling.

When you first arrive at the hospital, it can seem like
a big, busy place with many people coming and going.
When you go there, you often have to ask for directions.

You'll probably go to a *waiting room* until it's your turn for the hospital receptionist to see you.

As soon as your turn comes, you'll get a bracelet with your name on it. It's called an *ID bracelet.* That's just a short way of saying identification bracelet. You'll need to wear that bracelet as long as you stay in the hospital. If someone wants to know your name, that person can ask you or just look at your bracelet. You'll be able to take the bracelet off as soon as you go home, if you want.

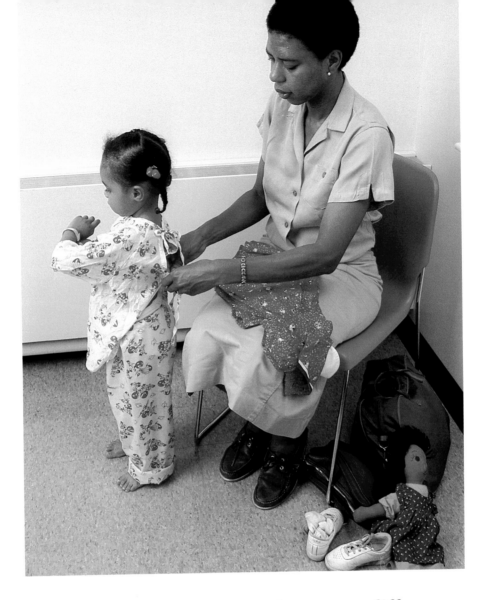

A person staying in the hospital may get a different
kind of pajamas or nightgown to wear . . . a kind that
doesn't have buttons, so it's easier to get in and out of.

The ID bracelet and the hospital pajamas may be new to you, but you'll see other things you might have seen before, either at home or in your doctor's office:

. . . the *scale* that you stand on to see how much you weigh and how tall you are;

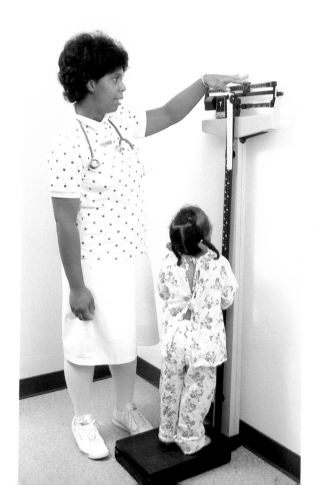

. . . the *thermometer* that takes your temperature;

. . . the *stethoscope* that lets the doctor listen to your breathing and heartbeat;

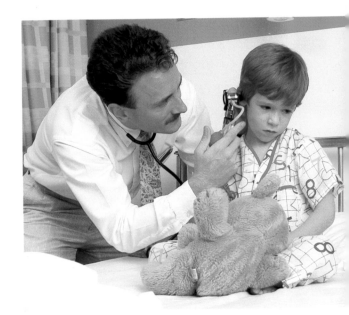

. . . the *otoscope* that helps the doctor see inside your ears, nose, or throat;

. . . the *blood pressure band* that gets tight on your arm and helps the doctor know more about how your heart is working.

One important way doctors learn how healthy you are is by looking at a little of your blood. That can be done by pricking your finger or using a small needle to take some blood out of your arm. It sometimes feels like a pinch, but the hurt goes away soon. And, of course, it's okay to cry if you want to. Your body is always making new blood, so you'll have plenty left.

Another way doctors learn about how healthy you are is by looking at some of your urine. It may seem strange to urinate in a cup, but that's what a doctor or nurse may need you to do.

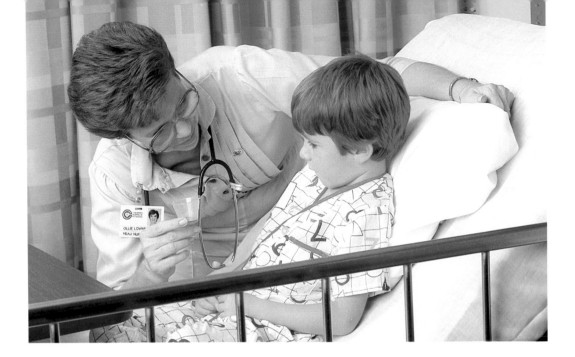

If you have to take some medicine while you are in the hospital, you might get it in a cup . . . or by a shot . . . or through an *IV*. An IV is a tiny needle connected to a small tube that can go in your hand or arm. The IV sends the medicine all through your body quickly and keeps it there as long as your body needs it.

Your doctor will know what kind of medicine you need and the best way to give it to you.

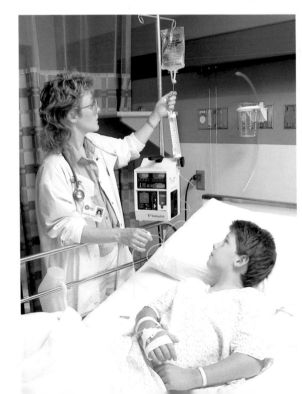

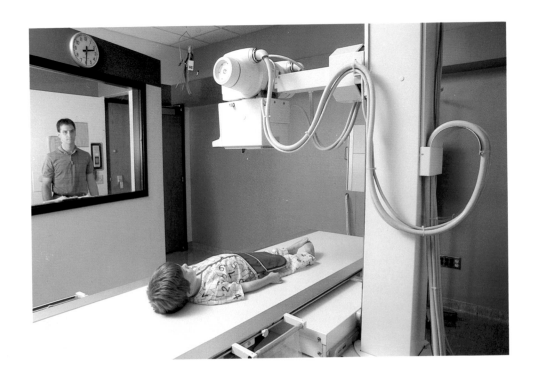

You might also go to a room where an *X-ray machine* takes pictures of the inside of your body. An X-ray table can feel cold and hard, and you have to stay very still for a moment while you hear the machine buzz.

Whoever's with you may have to stay just outside the door. X rays are over quickly, though, and just like any other pictures that people take, the X ray itself doesn't hurt.

Hospitals have special beds with sides that can go up to keep people from falling out. Everybody who has to be in the hospital sleeps in a bed like this—even grownups!

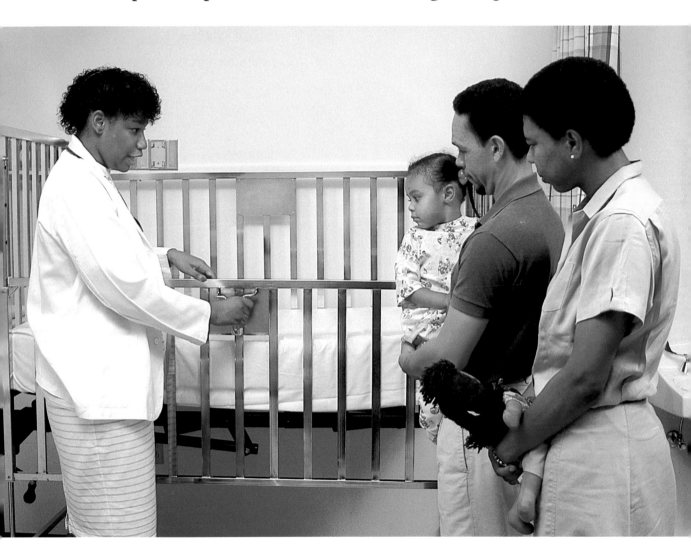

Some people get to eat in bed. That might be something they don't do at home, but it's all right to have meals in bed at the hospital. Someone will bring them to you on a tray that goes on a table that fits right over your bed.

At other times the table can come in handy as a place to draw and play.

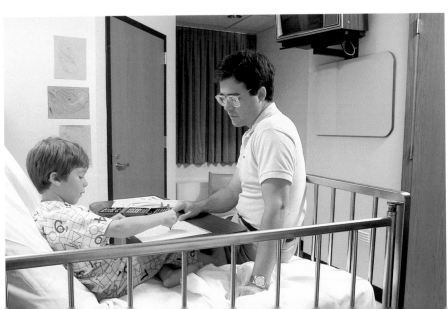

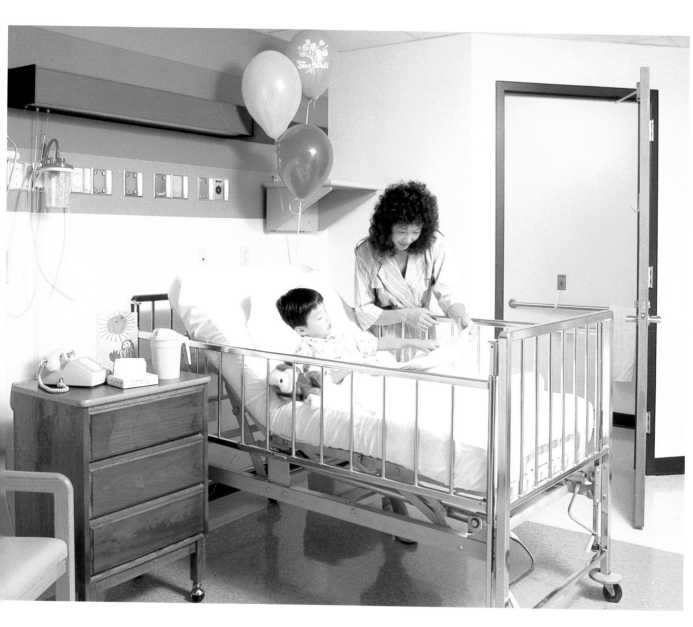

You may have a room all for yourself when
you stay in the hospital.

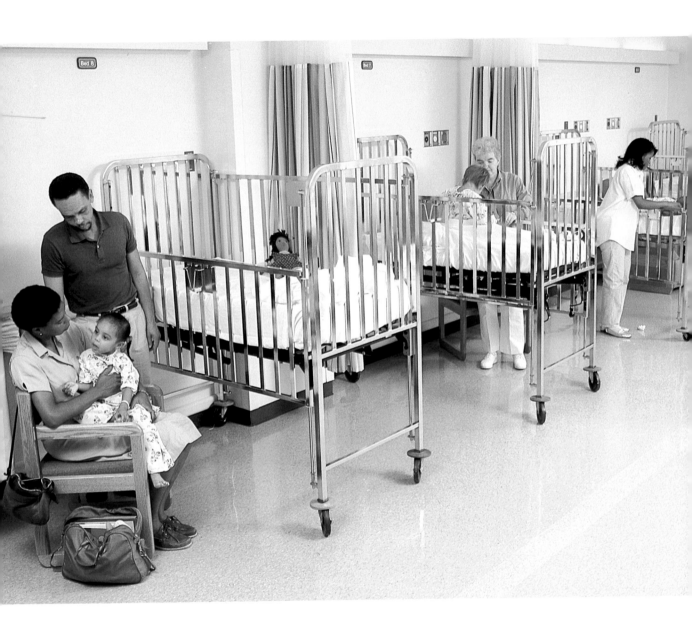

Or you may share a room with other children.

Some hospitals have rooms
where children can go to play.

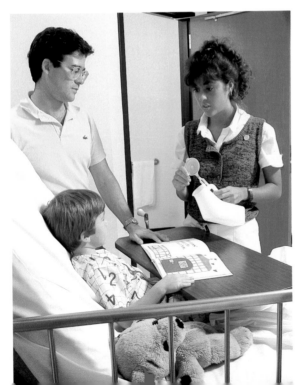

Hospitals have bathrooms, too. But if someone doesn't feel well enough to walk that far, a person can use a *bedpan* or *urinal*. It's a kind of toilet you can use right in your bed, and it doesn't get the bed wet or messy.

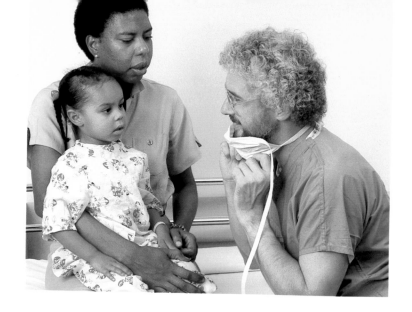

Nurses and doctors sometimes need to wear masks over their noses and mouths. But you'll still be able to see their eyes, and you can be sure they're still the same people underneath their masks—the same people who are helping you get well.

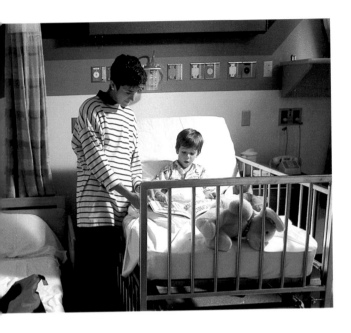

When children need to stay overnight in the hospital, their moms or dads sometimes stay with them, in the same room or a room nearby. But when moms and dads can't stay all the time, you can be sure that some nurses will be there all through the night.

It feels good to know that while you're in the hospital, there will always be someone who will listen if you have questions and who will come if you need help. Many people will be taking special care of you until you are well enough to go home.

And that's the best part: Going home to the place you know best and to the people you love the most . . . the ones who are so proud of how you're growing through hard times *and* easy times.